the tower of LONDON

APR/14

Author: Colin Hynson
Consultant: John Rogers

Copyright © *ticktock* Entertainment Ltd 2005

First published in Great Britain in 2005 by *ticktock* Media Ltd.,

Unit 2, Orchard Business Centre, North Farm Road, Tunbridge Wells, Kent, TN2 3XF

We would like to thank: Alison Howard, Susan Barraclough, Jenni Rainford and Elizabeth Wiggans for their help with this book.

ISBN 1 86007 599 1 PB

Printed in Hong Kong

A CIP catalogue record for this book is available from the British Library.

Contents

Introduction

The Tower of London is one of the most famous buildings in the world. Initially founded in 1066 as a mighty fortress to protect a new foreign king, it has served many purposes in its long history. The Tower has served as a royal residence, an armoury, home of the Royal Mint, a formidable and occasionally brutal prison and site of executions – and today, a dazzling tourist attraction.

A PARANOID KING?

King Edward the Confessor's death in January 1066 sparked a series of events that would change the course of English history. On his deathbed, the king was persuaded to pass the throne to his brother-in-law, Harold, Earl of Wessex. However, Edward may have promised Duke William of Normandy that he would let him become king. A furious William ordered his troops to invade England, and Harold was killed at the Battle of Hastings in 1066. William was crowned king at Westminster Abbey on Christmas Day.

The new King was faced with the daunting task of controlling a largely hostile population

This map from 1588 shows the Tower of London as it looked at that time, situated on the River Thames.

of over two million with an army of just 10,000 knights. To protect himself from attack William began a castle-building programme across the country. A wooden castle was hastily erected, but was soon pulled down to make way for an imposing new stone building which later became known as the White Tower.

TOWER EXPANSION

For the next 250 years, the Tower continued to grow at an impressive rate. By the early 14th century, the basic layout of the Tower that survives today had been achieved by the construction of two towered curtain walls and a moat. Henry III (1207–1272) and Edward I

The Battle of Hastings of 1066 is illustrated in detail in the Bayeux Tapestry. This scene from the famous artwork shows King Harold being killed.

(1272–1307) were the monarchs who had the greatest impact on the Tower's development. Until the 16th century, the Tower of London was the principal royal home. It was also the home of the Office of Armoury, the royal mint, the crown jewels and the monarch's personal zoo. But the Tower is perhaps best remembered as a prison and site of criminal executions. Famous people incarcerated at the Tower include: Henry VIII's second wife, Anne Boleyn; Sir Walter Raleigh; the Nazi war criminal Rudolf Hess and the notorious London gangsters the Kray twins. Today, the Tower of London is one of the most famous tourist attractions in the world, as millions of people visit this sprawling monument every year to see its many treasures for themselves.

The Tower of London, as it appears today. The vast complex of buildings has come a long way since the White Tower was built under the orders of William the Conqueror in the late 11th century.

CHAPTER 1

How it was built

S oon after William had been crowned King of England on Christmas Day in 1066, work began on the White Tower, the original Tower of London. The location for this new castle was chosen to take advantage of one of the strongest parts of the city wall left behind by the Romans. It also had the River Thames flowing beside it, which added another line of defence.

PRIME LOCATION

The choice of position for the Tower of London was not a difficult decision for William and his military advisors. The Roman city of Londinium had been surrounded by stone walls up to six metres in height. One of the strongest and most important parts of this wall was on a small hill overlooking the River Thames in the southeastern corner of the city. This was obviously the best place for William to build his main castle in London. He could use part of the Roman wall to strengthen the castle and it would be the first building seen by any ship sailing up the Thames.

MATERIALS

The original castle was completed quickly. Like nearly all of the castles built by William it was made of wood and earth. However, William knew that this could only be a temporary structure. He needed a more

This illustration from a 13th-century French manuscript shows how labourers transported blocks of stone up ramps for building.

permanent castle made of stone. Not only would this make it stronger and easier to defend but by using stone it sent out the message that William and the Normans were in England for good. In 1067 the timber rampart was pulled down so that a new,

stronger castle could be built in its place. The King chose the Bishop of Rochester, Gundulf, well-known for designing churches and castles in France, to be the architect. Although little is known about when work on the Tower began and finished, building was well advanced by the time of William's death in 1087. The fact that the Tower's first prisoner came to the Tower in 1100 also suggests that the building must have been completed by that time.

Building a castle of timber and earth was quick and easy and did not require a great deal of skill or labour. However, building a stone castle like the White Tower took many years to complete. If nothing was available locally, building material had to be brought in and both skilled and unskilled labour organised. All of this was organised by the king's officials alongside skilled builders called master masons. Other skilled workers like blacksmiths and carpenters had to be brought in as well. The unskilled work was done by gangs of local Anglo-Saxons who were probably not paid for their labour.

BUILDING THE TOWER

The first job that had to be done was to see if the ground could support such a large building. Since it was so close to the River Thames, the ground was very soft. Therefore, before the White Tower was built, trenches up to 15 feet deep were dug and filled with rubble. This provided the support for a plinth on which the Tower would be built. As the walls of the Tower began to rise, it became necessary to put up scaffolding. As the Tower got higher and higher long poles were placed in special holes that were built into the walls. These poles were then tied together with rope. These holes , known as 'putlog holes' can still be seen in

Medieval masons are shown building a wall in this German manuscript from 1068.

the White Tower and in many other Norman castles.

The types of stone used for building the White Tower were the grey English limestone called Kentish Rag and a cream-coloured limestone from Caen, France. The stone would have been cut to the right size and shape at the quarry before being transported by boat to the building site. This would have been one of the great advantages of having a large river next to where the castle was being built – as having to transport such heavy material overland would have been a much more gruelling and time-consuming task. The mortar, a mixture of sand and lime used to cement the stones together, was probably made on the Tower's site.

Huge vats would have been built by the river, in which the mortar would be mixed. It could then be taken by wheelbarrow to the builders. Many of the tools used to build the Tower of London would not be all that different to what

These modern-day masonry tools would not have been too dissimilar to the tools used to build the Tower of London.

7

The Tower of London

would be found on a modern building site. Medieval pictures of castles and cathedrals being built show that plumblines, wheelbarrows, chisels and drills were being used. Human-powered cranes were used to haul stones up to where they were needed.

CHANGING CASTLES

The earliest castles in England were built in the 'motte and bailey' style. This kind of castle included a fortified structure situated on a mound of earth (this was where the lord or king lived). The structure was surrounded by a defence wall which led down the hill and enclosed the castle buildings at the foot of the hill. The initial reason for the emergence of these castles was to offer some kind of defence to villagers who were being terrorised by raiders. However, these wooden castles soon proved to be inadequate fortresses – being vulnerable to fire and simply rotting from the weather – and so were replaced by stone castles. Various different styles of stone castle were built thereafter – attempting different shapes and building materials all with a view to increasing security. Then, the late 13th century saw

In the early medieval period, 'Motte and Bailey' castles (above) were the common style in Europe. The castle itself was made of wood and built on a mound (or 'motte') while the rest of the castle buildings were built on the flat. When William I became king, he recognised that a wooden castle was not going to be secure enough. His fortress was added to over time to become a 'concentric' castle as in the example below.

the rise of the 'concentric castle' – where an interior dwelling for the royalty or nobility was protected by many rings of walls; the inner walls being higher than the outer ones. The Tower of London that visitors see today has grown and changed in many ways since the White Tower was completed. These changes reflect the emergence of the improved architectural styles and methods of fortification.

EARLY EXPANSION

The first king to make major changes to the Tower was Richard I (1189–99). When he left England to take part in the Crusades, he left his Chancellor, William Longchamp, in charge of the kingdom. Longchamp began an ambitious building programme at the Tower of London. By the end of the 12th century, the area covered by the Tower had doubled. This was done by digging new ditches and building new walls, with a new tower (the Bell Tower) at the southwest corner. In the 1220s, the boy king Henry III began a major expansion of the Tower. He improved the kitchen and great hall, and built two towers next to the river – the Wakefield Tower and the Lanthorn Tower. Then, in the 1230s, Henry had a new wall containing nine towers built at the east, west, north and southeast sides of the Tower. Between 1275 and 1285 Edward I created a new wall outside the existing wall and a bigger moat. He also built the Beauchamp and St. Thomas' Towers. The first two Tudor monarchs also made many changes to the Tower.

MEDIEVAL RENAISSANCE

A number of changes were made to the Tower in the 19th century. The Waterloo Barracks were put up to accommodate 1,000 soldiers and many elements of the Tower were either restored, rebuilt or pulled down. During this period it was popular to restore elements of the Tower to their original styles. In 1852 the Beauchamp Tower was restored with a medieval appearance.

Similarly, the Salt Tower, the White Tower, St Thomas' Tower and the Bloody Tower were all renovated, while the Lanthorn Tower was rebuilt. Much of what appears to be original are actually Victorian restorations.

This reconstruction of the Tower of London shows how it would have looked in 1200. The additions by Richard I and William Longchamp are clearly visible – chiefly, the addition of new sections of curtain wall and the massive Bell Tower in the foreground.

Tales & customs – A RESTLESS QUEEN

The ghost of Anne Boleyn (Henry VIII's second wife) has been reportedly seen at the Tower more than any other. According to eyewitness accounts, she normally appears as a headless figure near the Queen's House. She has been identified through the period and style of her clothes. She has also been seen heading a procession of nobles in the Chapel of St. Peter ad Vincula.

The Tower was not primarily intended to be a castle that protected the people of London from attack. Neither was it supposed to be the principal place where the kings and queens of England would live – although many monarchs did in fact occasionally live there. It was initially built to provide a symbol of royal power and to serve as an easily defendable place for the royal family to shelter during periods of unrest.

THE FIRST SIEGE

The first known attack on the Tower took place during the reign of Richard I in 1191. King Richard spent many years away from his kingdom fighting in the Third Crusade. During this time, he left England in the hands of his chancellor, William Longchamp who ordered a massive expansion of the Tower. Richard's younger brother Prince John saw Longchamp as a barrier to his taking the English throne for himself. He therefore laid siege to the Tower in order to get rid of Longchamp. The new defences held up against this attack but Longchamp had to surrender when food in the Tower ran out.

Wat Tyler, the leader of the Peasants' Revolt of 1381 was eventually apprehended and killed, as illustrated here.

NOBLE REBELLION

When King John died in 1216, his nine-year old son Henry III, took the throne. At the time, much of the country was ruled over by nobles who had rebelled against King John. The Tower was actually controlled by an ally of the rebellious nobles, Prince Louis of France. It was not until 1217 that Henry III drove Louis out – so that he could take control of his country and his most important castle. Twice in the 1230s, Henry had to face rebellions by England's nobles. Both times he retreated to the Tower for safety. It was as a result of relying on the Tower that he began a massive expansion of

1066   William, Duke of Normandy, becomes King of England.

1067   Wooden castle built on the site of the Tower.

c. 1078   Work on the White Tower begins.

1101   The Tower's first prisoner, Ranulf Flambard, escapes.

1191   First known attack on the Tower.

1238   King Henry III's expansion of the Tower begins.

1241   White Tower is whitewashed.

1275–1285   King Edward I continues with improvements to the Tower.

1381   Peasants' Revolt forces King Richard II to shelter in the Tower.

the Tower's defences in the 1230s. Edward III was the last English king to begin a major building programme at the Tower. His father, Edward II, was forced to give up the throne by Parliament in 1327 and his 17-year-old son, Edward III, took the throne. His reign was peaceful and he made some improvements to the Tower defenses, such as rebuilding parts of the Bloody Tower.

PEASANTS' REVOLT

The Peasants' Revolt of 1381 was one of the largest rebellions in English history. The revolt was caused by the introduction of a hugely unpopular type of poll tax. King Richard II and his family sheltered in the Tower as up to 20,000 rebels ransacked London. The rebels actually took control of the Tower for a short while, killed several of the king's

In 1483, the 12-year-old rightful heir to the throne, Edward V, and his younger brother were imprisoned in the Tower of London. They disappeared shortly afterwards and were never seen again.

1455–1487   Wars of the Roses.
1465   King Edward IV holds lavish courts at the Tower.
1471   King Henry VI is murdered at the Tower.
1483   'The Princes in the Tower' disappear.

The Wars of the Roses, which occurred between 1455 and 1487, were the result of two rival noble families fighting for the throne.

closest advisors and looted his apartments. The revolt ended when the king promised to meet the people's demands. However, he never had any intention of keeping his promises.

WARS OF THE ROSES

The medieval period came to a close after a long series of civil wars between 1455–87, known as the Wars of the Roses. The Wars of the Roses were fought between the two noble families of Lancaster and York, both of whom claimed the throne. The Tower again played a key role in this period. Two kings were both killed there in mysterious circumstances during the Wars of the Roses – Henry VI in 1471 and Edward V in 1483. The civil wars came to an end with the death of the Richard III in 1485 and the arrival of the first Tudor king, Henry VII. From now the Tower became less a place of royal protection and

Henry VIII created the Protestant Church of England when he broke from the Roman Catholic Church in the 1530s.

more a prison for those who opposed the monarch.

RELIGIOUS RIFTS

Both Henry VII and Henry VIII made improvements to the Tower. However, the main improvements made by both made were more aesthetic than practical, that is – focused on making the royal lodgings more comfortable rather than improving the Tower's defences. This shows how confident the first Tudor kings

were that they would not have to face the same kind of rebellions endured by the medieval monarchs. In the 1530s, Henry VIII began to pull the English Catholic Church away from the control of the Pope in Rome and to create a new Protestant Church. This break was caused by Henry wanting to divorce his first wife, Catherine of Aragon, as she did not bear him a son, so that he could marry Anne Boleyn. The Pope refused to give his permission for the divorce to go ahead. This division caused religious conflict in England and the Tower was used by Tudor monarchs as a place to deal with those who opposed them. Henry VIII made several such people prisoners in the Tower.

UNJUST EXECUTIONS

In 1535, two of Henry VIII's most important advisers – Sir Thomas More and the Bishop of Rochester – were executed for refusing to

As did her father Henry VIII, when Elizabeth I became queen, she ordered many important Catholic figures to be imprisoned in the Tower.

accept Henry as the new head of the English Church. In May, 1536, Henry used the Tower to imprison and execute his second wife, Anne Boleyn. In 1542 Catherine Howard, Henry's fifth wife, was also executed in the Tower. Before the Catholic Mary I, Henry VIII's oldest daughter, came to the throne in 1553, she had to deal with an attempt to put Henry's Protestant great-niece, Lady Jane

Grey, on the throne. Jane was executed at the Tower in 1554. Mary then brought the English Church back to Catholic control. Like her father before her, she met resistance to this and the Tower was used to imprison those who defied her.

RESISTANCE TO THE MONARCH

Unlike her half-sister, Mary, and her father, Henry VIII, Elizabeth I was reluctant to execute her political and religious enemies. She preferred to rule with the support of as many of her subjects as she could get. However, that did not stop her using the Tower as a place to imprison those who resisted her rule and executions were ordered when she saw it as necessary. In 1601, just two years before her death, Robert Devereux, the Earl of Essex, was imprisoned and beheaded at the command of Elizabeth after he led a rebellion against her. Elizabeth died childless and the English throne was passed to the Scottish King, James. During his reign the relationship between the monarch and parliament began to worsen. When James' son, Charles I, inherited the throne, that relationship eventually broke down into civil war in 1642. In 1643 Parliament took control of the Tower to help defend of London. The civil war ended in 1649 when Charles I was executed. England was now a republic controlled

Henry VIII used the Tower of London as a place of imprisonment and execution for anyone who dared oppose him. Two of his six wives were sentenced to live their final days there before they were executed.

the Tower to store munitions and to provide workshops. The largest building was the Grand Storehouse which was erected in 1688. The Tower was used as a store for weapons until the start of World War I in 1914. Also during the reign of Charles II, the Crown Jewels began to be on display to the visiting public. The jewels

Charles II placed cannons in front of the Tower facing the River Thames. It was clear he would not hesitate to retaliate against an attack from any source, including his own people.

Coins were produced at the Tower's Royal Mint until the early 19th century. The Royal Mint is now situated in Wales.

by Oliver Cromwell. Cromwell was the first ruler of England to place soldiers in the Tower on a permanent basis.

A MESSAGE OF MILITARY MIGHT

In 1660, two years after the death of Oliver Cromwell in 1658, Charles I's son (also called Charles) returned from exile and assumed the throne of England and Scotland. Like Cromwell, Charles II believed that the Tower was the key to controlling London. It was under Charles II that cannon were first placed on the walls facing both the River Thames and towards the city. The message to the people of London was clear. If necessary, the Tower would be used by the king against his rebellious subjects. Several new buildings were put up inside

Time line

1674	Skeletons of two boys are discovered and are believed to be those of the 'Two Princes'.
1780	Last executions on Tower Hill.
1810	The Royal Mint is removed from the Tower.
1820s	The Tower is no longer used as a regular prison.
1826	The Duke of Wellington becomes Constable of the Tower.
late-1830s	Emergence of the Chartist movement.
1835	The Menagerie is removed from the Tower.

were moved to a new site in what is now called the Martin Tower.

ANIMALS AND MONEY

The Tower was, for several centuries, the home of the menagerie. While it may well have been King John who first introduced exotic animals to the Tower, it was his son Henry III who really developed the Tower Menagerie. Henry III owned an elephant, leopards and a polar bear. By the 1500s the animals in the menagerie had become an important tourist attraction. James I was fond of watching animal

fights and came to the Tower to view different animals fighting each other. In the early 1830s, William IV moved the animals out of the Tower to the new London Zoo.

The Tower was originally the site of the Royal Mint, where coins were first made during the reign of Edward I. Originally, blocks of gold and silver were cut into discs and stamped with the royal insignia. Machinery was introduced to the Mint under Charles II which meant that coins could be produced much faster.

By the end of the 1700s it was clear that there was not enough space at the Tower for the Mint. A new Mint outside the Tower began operating in 1812.

VICTORIAN TIMES

In the 1840s the Chartist movement shook London. The Chartists were calling for major political reform, including extending the vote to all adult men. England's rulers were nervous of the Chartists and decided to make the Tower an easier place to defend. Between 1848 and 1852, new gun

Throughout history and up to the present day, important state occasions have taken place at the Tower of London. In this picture, a military band performs before the queen in the courtyard of the Tower.

The Tower of London

This 19th century painting depicts the fire of 1841 that razed the Grand Storehouse completely to the ground. Queen Victoria's husband Prince Albert ordered for the Waterloo Barracks to be built in its place.

emplacements and a north bastion were added to strengthen the Tower against attack. In 1841, a fire swept through the Grand Storehouse at the Tower of London. The Waterloo Barracks were built on the site of the Grand Storehouse. The Barracks were built to house 1,000 soldiers. When the Chartist threat had died down, the country appeared to be at peace again – and so the Tower took on a different role. The last part of the Victorian period saw a huge increase in visitors to the Tower, since sightseers were first admitted in 1660. In 1841 the first official guidebook to the Tower was published and ten years later a purpose-built ticket office was erected. By the end of Queen Victoria's reign in 1901, half a million people were visiting the Tower each year.

WARTIME PRISONERS

In the 20th century, England fought in two world wars and the Tower of London once again became a place to imprison and execute enemies of the state. At the beginning of World War I (1914–1918), 11 German spies were imprisoned in the

Prince Albert, as shown in this 19th century painting, was responsible for a great proportion of the changes to the Tower during Queen Victoria's reign.

Time line

1841	The Grand Storehouse is destroyed by fire.		1852	Beauchamp Tower restored.
1841	The first official guidebook to the Tower published.		1870	Crown Jewels moved to Wakefield Tower.
1843	Queen Victoria orders the moat to be drained.		1914–1916	Eleven German spies executed at the Tower.
1845	Building work begins on Waterloo Barracks.		1939	Tower closed to the public and the Crown Jewels removed.
1850s	Tower heavily restored.			

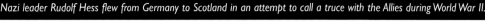
Nazi leader Rudolf Hess flew from Germany to Scotland in an attempt to call a truce with the Allies during World War II.

Tower and later executed by firing squad inside the Tower. Unlike many other parts of London, the Tower did not suffer from any bomb damage during World War I. Only one bomb landed harmlessly in the moat.

The Tower suffered much more bomb damage during World War II. The bastion built on the northern wall to defend the Tower against the Chartists was hit, along with some other 19th century buildings. During World War II the Tower was closed to the public and the Crown Jewels were taken to a secret location.

Everybody was encouraged to grow their own food and even the moat of the Tower was used for this purpose. World War II saw the last execution at the Tower when a German spy named Josef Jakobs was shot in 1941. The chair that he sat in when he faced the firing squad was put on public display for many years. During World War II the Tower became most famous as the prison of Rudolf Hess. Hess was very close to Adolf Hitler and a very important member of the German government. In 1941 he flew a plane across to Scotland in a desperate attempt to negotiate peace between Britain and Germany. The British government refused and placed him under arrest inside the Tower. He was held at the Tower for four days until he was sent to Nuremberg in Germany for trial and placed in prison (see also p. 33).

POST-WAR PEACE

At the end of the war the Tower of London returned to its peaceful role of a top tourist destination. However, in 1952 the Tower briefly became a prison once more for some high-profile prisoners. This would be one of the last times the Tower was used for this purpose. The infamous gangsters known as the Kray Twins were called up to start their National Service in the army. When they failed to turn up they were arrested by the police and taken to the Waterloo Barracks, where they were held overnight. They then spent the next two years either on the run from the army or in military prison.

1941   German deputy Rudolf Hess temporarily imprisoned in the Tower after he attempted to fly from Germany to Scotland – allegedly to negotiate an end to World War II.

1946   Tower reopened to the public.

1948   Crown Jewels returned to the Tower.

The function of the Tower of London has changed greatly over the centuries of its existence. Each of its buildings has a unique function and legendary status. The Tower was not primarily intended to act as London's primary symbol of military might – however, the tower and all of its components have managed to stand for nearly 1,000 years, and will continue to stand for years to come. Read the following pages for a closer look – inside and out!

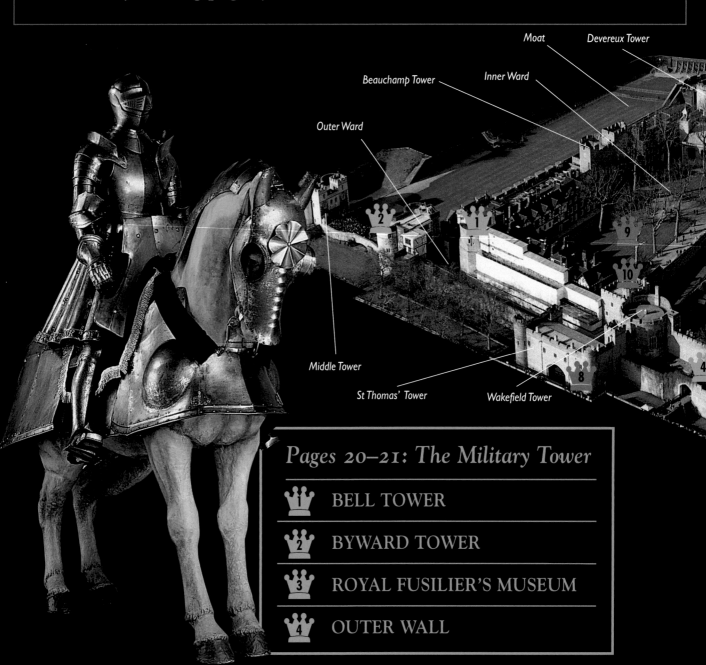

Moat

Devereux Tower

Beauchamp Tower

Inner Ward

Outer Ward

Middle Tower

St Thomas' Tower

Wakefield Tower

Pages 20–21: The Military Tower

♕ 1 BELL TOWER

♕ 2 BYWARD TOWER

♕ 3 ROYAL FUSILIER'S MUSEUM

♕ 4 OUTER WALL

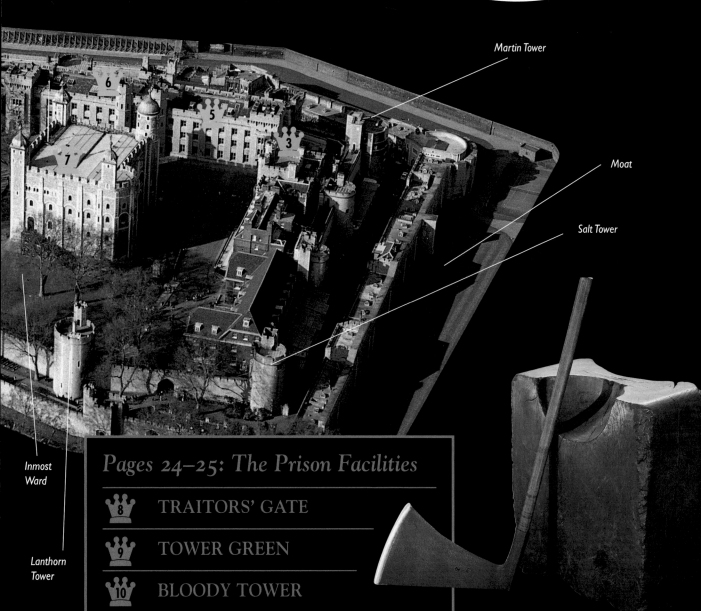

Martin Tower

Moat

Salt Tower

Inmost Ward

Lanthorn Tower

♛ BELL TOWER

The **BELL TOWER** is situated at the southwest corner of the Inner Ward. Built in the 13th century, the Bell Tower earned its name from having the 'belfry' at the top. Historically, the bell was rung as an alarm but today, it is only rung to advise visitors when closing time is approaching.

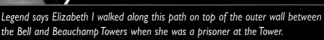

Legend says Elizabeth I walked along this path on top of the outer wall between the Bell and Beauchamp Towers when she was a prisoner at the Tower.

♛2 BYWARD TOWER

It is possible to enter the Tower via the Middle Tower, then across a drawbridge to the **BYWARD TOWER**. The Byward Tower originally had two portcullises (huge wooden grills, which could be raised or lowered). If you look up as you pass through the archway you will see a series of 'murder holes'. Legend states that defenders of the Tower could use these holes to pour boiling oil on attackers. However, they were more likely to have been used to douse fires.

The twin-towered gatehouse known as the Byward Tower was built during the reign of Edward I.

The Tower of London houses two collections of military artifacts. The first is in the White Tower; and the second is housed in the Royal Fusilier's Museum (above), which was established in 1685.

♛₃ ROYAL FUSILIER'S MUSEUM

On the east side of the fortress is a 19th century building that houses the **ROYAL FUSILIERS MUSEUM**. The Royal Regiment of Fusiliers was founded by James II (1685–1688) in 1685 in order to protect the royal guns inside the Tower. The Regiment has been involved in many military campaigns including the American War of Independence, the Boer War, both World War I and World War II and the first Gulf War. Memorabilia from these campaigns is on show in this museum.

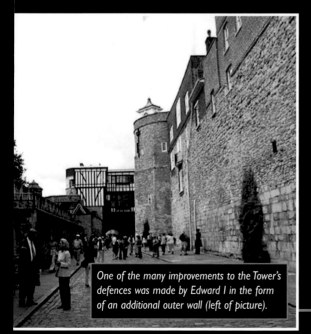

One of the many improvements to the Tower's defences was made by Edward I in the form of an additional outer wall (left of picture).

♛₄ OUTER WALL

When visitors walk into the Tower, they will see that it is defended by two walls. Some of the inner wall was built by William Longchamp, Chancellor to Richard I (1189–99). Between 1275 and 1285 Edward I added an entirely new **OUTER WALL** in order to make the Tower of London a near-impregnable fortress. Invaders could not get in and royal prisoners could not get out.

The Waterloo Barracks were built in 1845 and replaced the Grand Storehouse which was destroyed by a fire in 1841. The cannons in front of the building were captured from the French at the Battle of Waterloo.

WATERLOO BARRACKS

The **WATERLOO BARRACKS** were built in the 19th century while the Duke of Wellington was Constable of the Tower. The Barracks were intended as an accommodation block for about 1,000 soldiers. They were designed in the neo-gothic style, which reflects how much people in the 19th century admired medieval styles. The building was named after the Battle of Waterloo and defeat of Napoleon in 1815.

THE CROWN JEWELS

Today, the Waterloo Barracks is the home of the **CROWN JEWELS**. The Crown Jewels have been on display to the public since the 17th century. They have been in different parts of the Tower since the 14th century, except during World War II when they were moved to a secret location.

The crown Jewels are currently located in the Jewel House in the Waterloo Barracks.

WHITE TOWER

The building with the strongest royal connection and the earliest existing structure in the Tower of London is the **WHITE TOWER**. It took about 30 years to build and was completed by 1100 during the reign of William II. It is called the White Tower because it was whitewashed when Henry III was king. The main entrance is through a door on the ground floor.

The oldest building at the Tower of London, the White Tower gained its name from when Henry III had it whitewashed in the 13th century.

Displays throughout the **WHITE TOWER** are from the Royal Armouries collection. The collection includes weapons for the armed forces from the medieval period right up until the start of World War One. This collection of weaponry dates from the reign of Henry VIII, right up until recent times. Notable pieces in the collection are the armour of Henry VIII and Edward I, and the Spanish Armoury contains the Tower's torture instruments.

The Chapel of St. John the Evangelist in the White Tower was where the Royal family and court worshipped. It was built during the Norman period.

On the first floor are rooms that were used by kings and queens for entertaining and for important royal events. One room that was used for many such occasions is the **CHAPEL OF ST. JOHN THE EVANGELIST**. Here the body of the wife of Henry VII lay after her death. Henry VIII's daughter, Mary I, married King Philip of Spain here in 1554, even though Philip was not actually present at the time. It was used as a chapel in medieval times but from the 16th to the 19th centuries, it was used to store records of state.

The Tower of London

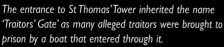
The entrance to St Thomas' Tower inherited the name 'Traitors' Gate' as many alleged traitors were brought to prison by a boat that entered through it.

TRAITORS' GATE

The watergate entrance to the Tower has been known as **'TRAITORS' GATE'** since the 17th century. Although originally built so that the king or queen would have an easier access route to the Tower, the gate gained its name because of the number of prisoners accused of treason who were brought into the Tower via this entrance. The gate is located beneath St Thomas' Tower and was built by Edward I in the 13th century.

TOWER GREEN

The main open area of the Tower of London is known as **TOWER GREEN**. Tower Green was a private open space for about 300 years. Before this, Tower Green was the site of seven private executions in the 15th and 16th centuries. Private executions were reserved for the most important prisoners. Amongst the prisoners whose lives ended there were Anne Boleyn, Catherine Howard and Lady Jane Grey. Today a plaque stands in the place where the scaffold stood, recognising the lives that ended there.

Built in the 13th century, the Bloody Tower was a part of the Tower that was used as a prison. It was believed that the two princes were murdered here, and it is because of this that the Tower earned its rather grisly name. The reality is, however, that the princes probably weren't held here.

🔟 THE BLOODY TOWER

Before St. Thomas' Tower was built there was another tower that sat on the edge of the River Thames and served as the gateway between the river and the Tower. This tower is now known as the **BLOODY TOWER**. Some of the stories and legends that emerged from the Tower were supposed to have taken place in the Bloody Tower. The Bloody Tower was first built in the 1220s with a new floor added in about 1360, during the reign of Edward III.

Parts of the Bloody Tower are decorated to represent different historical periods, and these displays are often updated. This bed (above) is a replica of the one slept in by Sir Walter Raleigh when he was a prisoner in the Tower.

The Bloody Tower was designed to provide comfortable accommodation with a fireplace, tiled floor and large windows. It was usually set aside as a guest room for anybody visiting the Constable of the Tower. However, it was also used as a place to keep some of the more important prisoners, such as Sir Walter Raleigh, who spent 13 years in these lodgings.

CHAPTER 4

The people

The Tower of London has always been linked with the English, and later the British, monarchy. The monarchs saw the Tower as a symbol of their strength and prestige. They used the Tower to control the often-rebellious population of London, to imprison their political and religious enemies, as a place to retreat to in times of strife and as a place of entertainment. Nearly every king and queen has left some kind of mark on the history of the Tower – including ordering many famous historical figures to be imprisoned, and even executed, there.

WILLIAM THE CONQUEROR

The monarch who started building the Tower of London was William I (also known as William the Conqueror). He built the original Tower after he had taken the crown by force. His victory in 1066 at the Battle of Hastings led to England having a new royal family, a new style of building, a new language and new set of rulers. He was a brilliant and ruthless military leader. He managed to hold on to his lands despite rebellions from within and invasions from the outside. One such invasion was led by the king of France. When William invaded England, he had planned to keep many of the English nobles in their place. However, continuing resistance to his taking the English crown meant that he replaced the English nobles with reliable French-speaking nobles. He also built castles and cathedrals across the country to help maintain control over his new subjects. There are many

This detail from the 11th century work called the 'Bayeux Tapestry' shows soldiers heading off to join King Harold in the Battle of Hastings in 1066.

One of the earliest reported ghosts at the Tower was St. Thomas à Becket. It was said that when work on Traitor's Gate was nearly finished in 1240, a violent storm caused the gate to collapse. After the exact same thing happened a year later, a priest claimed to have seen the ghost of Sir Thomas à Becket striking the walls with a crucifix. The priest said that the ghost was proclaiming that the new building was not for the common good but 'for the injury and prejudice of the Londoners, my brethren'.

The Domesday Book was an account of all property owned in England in 1086. It has proved an invaluable resource for learning about people in the Middle Ages.

remarkable documents ever created in English history. At the end of 1085 William ordered that a record be made of all of the land and property in England. Agents were sent around the country and their findings were compiled in the Domesday Book.

great monuments to William's harsh rule in our towns and cities. However, William I was also responsible for one of the most

MERCILESS EDWARD

Another medieval monarch that had a great impact on the Tower was Edward I (1272–1307). No other monarch made such an effort to rule the whole of Britain. He conquered Wales and built a series of castles to defend his new kingdom. He also invaded Scotland on several occasions and managed to influence who was placed on the Scottish throne. The improvements that he made to the Tower was purely to make sure that he could keep control of his capital. He is also remembered

This illustration from a 13th century French manuscript shows Edward I (reigned 1272–1307) seated on his throne before his subjects.

as the monarch who expelled the Jews of England.

ROYAL EXECUTIONS

The most tragic members of the royal family to have a link with the Tower were the so-called 'Princes in the Tower'. When King Edward IV (1461–70 and 1471–83)

The Tower of London

This 16th century painting by Holbein captures the beauty of Anne Boleyn, second wife of Henry VIII. She was imprisoned for alleged adultery and beheaded on Tower Green in 1536.

died, his two sons, Edward and Richard, were taken to the Tower by their uncle, Richard (the deceased king's brother). Twelve-year-old Edward was supposed to have become Edward V but he was never crowned. Instead, his uncle was crowned Richard III in 1483 – as the two princes had mysteriously disappeared. There were rumours that Richard had ordered their murder – rumours that Richard made no attempt to deny. In 1674, two skeletons were discovered in the Tower. The size of the bones suggests that they could have been those of the two princes. The bones were transferred and buried in Westminster Abbey. In 1933 the marble urn in which the bones were placed was opened up for inspection. An examination of the bones concluded that they were the skeletons of two boys of the same age as the two princes were when they disappeared.

A KINGDOM DIVIDED

In Tudor times it was the larger-than-life figure of Henry VIII (1509–47) that meant that the Tower yet again played a major part in the history of England. From the 1520s, Henry was becoming increasingly worried that he did not have a son to take the throne when he died. He only had a daughter, Mary. He blamed his wife, Catherine of Aragon, for this and decided to marry Anne Boleyn instead. However, the Pope did not allow the king to divorce Catherine. Henry reacted by breaking the English Church from the Roman Catholic Church and setting himself up as the head of the Church in England. He could now divorce and marry again. Many objected to Henry's divorce and refused to acknowledge him as head of the Church. Henry reacted by having

Lady Jane Grey was executed in 1554 for undeservedly claiming a right to the throne.

Tales & customs – LIVES CUT SHORT

The spirits of the 'Two Princes' have occasionally been reported as being seen in the Bloody Tower, where they were believed to have been imprisoned. They are said to be wearing white nightgowns and are holding hands. However, if the observor dared approach, they would apparently shrink into the wall and disappear. Yeoman Warders have reported hearing the sound of a child crying in buildings called the Casemates, which are around the outer walls of the Tower. Those who heard the sound always investigated but found nothing.

Sir Thomas More and the Bishop of Rochester arrested and placed in the Tower. They were both executed in 1535.

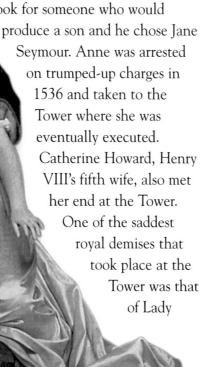

INNOCENT WOMEN

Henry VIII's second wife also met an unhappy end in the Tower. She had married Henry in 1533. In the same year she gave birth to Elizabeth. Again Henry began to look for someone who would produce a son and he chose Jane Seymour. Anne was arrested on trumped-up charges in 1536 and taken to the Tower where she was eventually executed. Catherine Howard, Henry VIII's fifth wife, also met her end at the Tower. One of the saddest royal demises that took place at the Tower was that of Lady

This 19th century painting shows the 'Two Princes' who mysteriously disappeared in the Tower. It is widely believed they were murdered.

Jane Grey. When Edward VI died in 1553 England had completed its break with the Roman Catholic Church and had become a Protestant country. The new monarch was the Catholic Mary I. She was determined to return the Church to the arms of Rome. Protestant nobles conspired to put Lady Jane Grey, the great-niece of Henry VIII, on the throne. For nearly two weeks they appeared to be successful. However, a series of

The Tower of London

uprisings propelled Mary on to the throne. Lady Jane Grey, who was never more than a pawn in a game, was subsequently arrested and placed in the Tower. She was executed there in February 1554.

A COMFORTABLE PRISON?

The Tower of London has been used as a prison for most of its history. Many of the prisoners were not jailed for any crimes that they actually committed but because they had somehow earned the displeasure of the reigning monarch. The Tower gained the reputation as a grim and foreboding prison. However, for many prisoners, so long as they had enough money to pay for it, prison life inside the Tower could be quite comfortable. The first recorded prisoner was Ranulf Flambard, the Bishop of Durham. He was put in the Tower in 1100 by Henry I after he was accused of extortion. Flambard lived in some style in the White Tower. He had his own servants and had many visitors from the outside world. On February 2, 1101, he threw a party for his guards. He allowed the guards to drink as much wine as they wanted. That evening, as the guards were deep in a drunken sleep, he lowered a rope out the window, climbed down to the

Sir Thomas More was Lord Chancellor when Henry VIII wanted to divorce his first wife, Catherine, so he could marry Anne Boleyn. More resigned from his post and was subsequently imprisoned and executed outside the Tower on Tower Hill.

ground and made his getaway. That not only made him the first known prisoner of the Tower but also the first to make an escape.

NOT-SO-LUCKY ESCAPE

Besides the members of the English royal family to be imprisoned in the Tower, certain non-English royalty also spent time there as prisoners. The Welsh prince, Llewelyn ap Gruffydd, was imprisoned by Henry III. In 1244, Gruffydd tried to escape from the Tower on a rope. Sadly, the rope broke and he fell to his death. It was written that when he was found, 'his head and neck were driven into his breast, between the shoulders'.

HIGH PROFILE PRISONERS

The most notable foreign prince who was imprisoned in the Tower was Charles, Duke of Orleans. He was captured at the Battle of Agincourt in 1415. In those days, prisoners were often held for money. They would be freed after a ransom was paid. Charles was a prisoner in England for 25 years before his ransom was

The Tower of London has seen hundreds of prisoners since 1100. The details of each have been recorded in The Book of Prisoners.

Tales & customs – STRANGE SCENTS

Several visitors and staff have reported smelling something strange in the Chapel of St. John in the White Tower. The smell is described as a strong perfume like incense and is strongest at night. Most strange of all, in 1817 the Keeper of the Crown Jewels, Edmund Swifte, and his family were having supper in the Martin Tower. Suddenly Edmund Swifte and his wife saw a strange cylinder filled with a white and blue liquid move around the room and then slowly fade away into the wall.

eventually paid. It was rumoured that during his long days in the Tower, Charles turned to writing poetry. After his release, it was said that Henry VII had the Duke's poetry bound into a book which Henry presented to his bride, Elizabeth of York. The book also contained several painted pictures, called 'illuminations'.

This illumination from the Duke of Orleans' book of poems shows him as a prisoner in the Tower. This picture is one of the earliest images of the Tower of London.

Under the Tudor kings and queens, many prisoners were in the Tower because they could not agree with the religious practices of their monarch. Under Henry VIII, Edward VI, Mary I and Elizabeth I, the Tower became a prison and place of death for many well-known religious figures. One of the most famous of these was Sir Thomas More. More was a well-

known scholar and writer. He opposed both Henry VIII's decision to divorce his first wife and to break with the Roman Catholic Church. In 1529 More became Lord Chancellor but he resigned in 1532 when he felt that he could no longer support Henry VIII's policies. He tried to live a quiet life after that but Henry saw

31

The Tower of London

Roman Catholic soldier Guy Fawkes was discovered trying to blow up Parliament. He was taken to the Tower and later executed.

him as a threat and had him imprisoned. After refusing to accept Henry as the new head of the English church he was executed on Tower Hill in 1535.

CAUGHT RED-HANDED

Guy Fawkes was another famous prisoner placed in the Tower. In November, 1605, a group led by Robert Catesby decided to end the persecution of Roman Catholics in England by blowing up James I and members of the Houses of Lords and Commons. The plot was uncovered and Guy Fawkes was discovered on November 4 under the parliament buildings with a large amount of gunpowder. He was immediately taken to the Tower as a prisoner. The warders at the Tower needed a confession

from Fawkes as well as more information about his fellow conspirators. On November 16, Fawkes signed his confession. His barely legible signature suggests that he was in an incredible amount of pain after being tortured into signing a confession. We still celebrate the failure of the Gunpowder Plot every year on November 5 with the lighting of fireworks.

ADVENTURER CONFINED

One of England's best-known sailors and explorers was Sir Walter Raleigh. He ended his days as a disgraced prisoner in the Tower.

The famous explorer Sir Walter Raleigh was first imprisoned in the Tower for marrying one of Elizabeth I's ladies-in-waiting.

In the 1580s Raleigh took part in a series of adventures and fought for Elizabeth I in Ireland between 1580–1. During this time he became one of the queen's favourites. In 1591 it was discovered that Raleigh was secretly married to one of the queen's ladies-in-waiting. Elizabeth flew into a jealous rage and had Raleigh thrown into the Tower. He was released after five weeks when he promised to share any treasure he captured from his expeditions. These expeditions often led to clashes with Spanish ships. Elizabeth I did not mind this too much, particularly after the failed Spanish Armada in 1588.

The new king, James I, was keen to make peace with

Rudolf Hess (right) was one of the highest-ranking members of Hitler's (left) Nazi Party. In 1941, Hess flew an aeroplane from Germany to Scotland. No-one knows for sure his reason for doing this but many believe he wanted to call a truce with the Allies. Instead he was captured and imprisoned in the Tower.

the Spanish and he had Raleigh imprisoned in the Tower for a second time in 1603, for allegedly conspiring against James I and trying to place the king's cousin, Lady Arabella Stuart, on the throne. This time Raleigh remained a prisoner at the Tower until 1616. During this time he conducted scientific experiments and wrote the first volume of his ambitious *History of the World*. His second child, Carew, was even baptised at St. Peter ad Vincula in 1605. Raleigh was eventually executed in 1618 at Westminster, after leading an unsuccessful expedition to find the legendary city of El Dorado in which he clashed again with the Spanish.

MODERN-DAY PRISON

The Tower of London was used continually as a prison until the 1820s. Just over 100 years later it was again used as a temporary prison for the Nazi war criminal Rudolf Hess. Hess was third in command to Adolf Hitler, the leader of Nazi, Germany. Hess was taken prisoner and temporarily put in the Tower. In 1945 Hess was tried for war crimes at Nuremberg in Germany. Hess was sentenced to life imprisonment. He died in 1987 at the age of 92 (see p. 17).

Tales & customs – THE ROAMING RALEIGH

Sightings of the ghost of Sir Walter Raleigh is one of those most commonly reported. It is believed by many that due to his long period of incarceration in the Tower and the amount of freedom given to him to walk around, that he may be coming back to visit old acquaintances. Several Yeomen have reported seeing him near the guardroom. He is said to appear in a very solid form and only ever remains for a short while.

CHAPTER 5

Tower traditions

Like many other ancient buildings, the Tower of London has many customs and traditions that are part of the story of the Tower. They range from the Yeoman Warders in their striking uniforms to the ravens that nest adjacent to the Wakefield Tower.

It is not known from when exactly ravens first lived at the Tower. The birds are tended by the raven-master who hand-rears them as babies.

WATCHING OVER THE TOWER

One of the best-known sights at the Tower are the Yeoman Warders. They are often called Beefeaters although the warders never use this name themselves. Historically, their job was to guard royal prisoners and the Tower gates. The red-and-gold uniform is only worn on special occasions, such as church parades or when an important visitor comes to the Tower. They normally wear a red and blue uniform (pictured right) that was introduced in 1858. Now that the prisoners are gone, the main duties of the Yeoman Warders are to look after the many tourists who visit the Tower. They are still, officially, bodyguards for the monarch. All Yeoman Warders must be former members of the armed forces with at least 22 years service. The Tower of London is also watched over by about 30 ravens. The birds are tended by a by one of the Yeoman Masters called a Ravenmaster.

CEREMONY OF THE KEYS

One of the most important ceremonies that the Yeoman Warders take part in happens every night when the Tower is closed. This is the Ceremony of the Keys when the Tower is locked and made secure. It has happened every night for hundreds of years. This probably makes it the oldest military ceremony in the world. Nobody

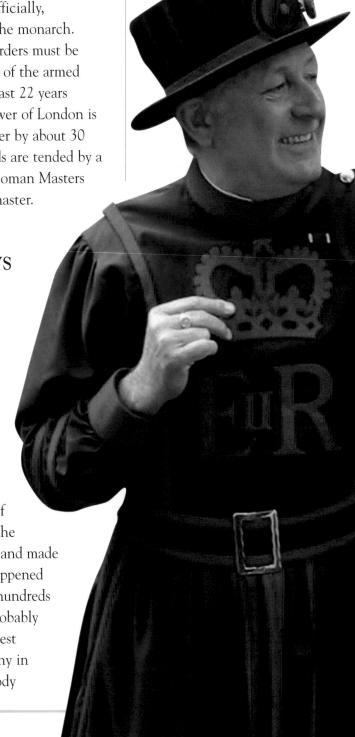

knows when the ceremony started but it probably dates right back to when the White Tower was built by William the Conqueror. The Ceremony of the Keys starts every night at 9.50 p.m. The Chief Yeoman Warder (accompanied by an armed guard) carries a lantern with a candle burning inside as he walks around the Tower. He uses the Queen's Keys to lock up all the gates on the outer walls before marching to the Bloody Tower, where the keys are handed over to the Resident Governor for safe-keeping.

St. Peter ad Vincula is the site of the 'Beating of the Bounds' ceremony that also takes place at parishes around the country on Ascension Day every three years.

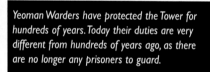

Yeoman Warders have protected the Tower for hundreds of years. Today their duties are very different from hundreds of years ago, as there are no longer any prisoners to guard.

OTHER CEREMONIES

Another important ceremony that takes place at the Tower is the Ceremony of Lilies and Roses. In 1471, Henry VI was supposedly murdered in the Oratory at Wakefield Tower. Every year on the anniversary of his death, school pupils from Eton and King's College place lilies and roses on the spot where he was killed. Henry VI had helped to found both the school and college.

The 'Beating of the Bounds' ceremony takes place every three years on Ascension Day, which is forty days after Easter. The earliest record of the Tower taking part in this custom dates back to at least 1381. The ceremony takes place outside the Tower. Thirty-one boundary stones that mark the Tower's boundary are beaten by local choirboys with long sticks or 'willow wands'. It is believed that, originally, during the 'beating of the bounds', children were beaten so that they would remember the borders of their parish.

Tales & customs – THE RAVENS

Nobody knows when the ravens first appeared at the Tower but they were soon protected by a legend that arose around them. It was believed that without them the Tower and entire country would fall. One of Charles II's astronomers complained that the ravens were interfering with his observations. The king ordered them to be killed. However, when he found out about the legend he allowed a small number to remain. Their wings were clipped to make sure that they did not fly away.

CHAPTER 6

Uncovering the past

Very little is known about the early history of the Tower. There are plenty of documents relating to the building of the Tower in the medieval period, but most of these are only accounts of the money spent on the construction, rather than information about building methods and cultural practices. What actually happened in the Tower in the first few centuries of its existence is also difficult to piece together, largely because the number of literate people during the Tudor period was far lower than today – meaning that written records were few.

This Iron Age skeleton was excavated in 1976 from a site near Lanthorn Tower (one of the Towers that faces the River Thames).

WHAT EXCAVATIONS HAVE TOLD US

Many gaps in the knowledge of historians have been filled by archaeological findings. There have been many archaeological digs in and around the Tower. Excavations in the 1960s and 1970s revealed much about the early history of the Tower and also what happened on the site before the arrival of the Normans. In 1976 a skeleton was discovered during an excavation close to the Lanthorn Tower. The skeleton was from the Iron Age – just before the arrival of the Romans in AD 43. Archaeologists believe that the skeleton belonged to a man who was buried before the Romans began to settle in what would eventually become the city of London.

EARLY CASTLES

When the Normans began their castle-building programme in England, they erected 'motte and bailey' castles. These were wooden structures consisting of a defensive wall surrounding a large building on top of a mound. The Tower of London, however, was different. The Romans had built three miles of stone walls around London. One of the largest and strongest

In the run-up to Halloween, 2001, a team of ghost hunters spent several nights in the Tower of London. Experts used temperature gauges, infra-red light and 'black cameras' that can see in the darkness. All of this equipment was trained on four of the Tower's most haunted locations, Sir Walter Raleigh's study in the Bloody Tower, the Bell Tower, the Chapel of St. Peter ad Vincula and the Beauchamp Tower. A live webcam allowed people around the world to watch out for ghostly apparitions. Nothing was seen or recorded during this time.

parts of this wall was where the Tower of London was built. Since it had the River Thames on one side and the Roman wall on

Evidence from archaeological digs have taught us a great deal about the Tower of London.

another, all William I had to do was build a ditch on the other sides. The buildings inside were then safe.

UNCOVERING THE EVIDENCE

Nobody knew exactly where these ditches were. This was important to know because it would tell historians how much space the first Tower of London actually took up. These ditches were eventually discovered during archaeological excavations in the 1960s. The foundations of Roman buildings have also been discovered both close to and underneath the White Tower.

ANCIENT TREES

One of the ways that archaeologists can date a building is through the science of 'dendrochronology'. This works by assessing the timber used in any building. As a tree grows upwards and outwards it leaves a ring in its trunk. Each ring represents one year's growth. There

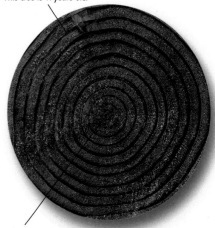

The number of rings represents the tree's age. This tree is 11 years old.

The centre ring indicates the earliest year of the tree's life.

> Dendrochronology is the study of the rings on the cross section of a tree to determine how old the tree is.

is still some debate about when work on the White Tower actually began. However, applying dendrochronology to the timbers in the White Tower shows that building was certainly under way by 1081.

RE-FLOODING THE MOAT

One of the most important Tower of London discoveries occurred between 1995 and 1997. For much of the Tower's history

Excavations, such as this one that took place in the moat outside the Develin Tower in 1997, have revealed many previously unknown facts about the Tower's history.

ensure that nothing of historical importance would be lost in the process. Therefore excavations needed to take place. As a consequence, the moat was not re-flooded and remains empty today.

TREES WITH HISTORY

When they dug in the western moat, near Beauchamp Tower, archaeologists discovered the remains of a high-quality building. It was known that Henry III had built an entrance to the Tower, but until 1995 nobody was sure of its exact location. Wooden piles around the building remains were found, which supported documentary evidence that a Tower building fell down in the mid-13th century. Dendrochronology dated these trunks to the winter of 1240 and 1241.

In 1956, this workman found two pieces of 18th century pottery during maintenance work near the Wakefield Tower..

the moat was filled with water from the nearby River Thames. The moat was drained and filled in during 1843 after the moat gained a reputation as a smelly and unhygienic place. In 1995 the project – called the Tower Environs Scheme – was launched. The idea of the scheme was to improve the appearance of the area around the Tower; to improve access for visitors and to re-flood the moat. Before proceeding, however, it was important to

Tales & customs – SPECIAL SALUTES

Ever since the invention of guns they have been fired in celebration as well as in war. These are known as 'salutes'. The Tower of London had one of the earliest salutes in England when guns were fired to celebrate the coronation of Anne Boleyn in 1533. Today the guns are fired to signal the birthdays of the Queen and her husband Prince Philip. They are also fired on the anniversary of the Queen coming to the throne and at the State Opening of Parliament.

The finding of this 15th century fish trap with the remains of a fish inside proved that fishing once took place in the moat.

TOWER MILLS

The presence of mills at the Tower was known from a document of 1276. This document mentions how 600 trees had been felled and brought to the Tower to act as the piles on which the mills would sit. Again, it was not known exactly where the mills were located until 1996 when archaeologists discovered a large number of tree trunks that had been driven into the river bed. It was proven that the trees were cut down in 1276 – the year the mills were built.

AN HISTORIC FISHING SPOT

One of the most interesting artifacts to be found in the moat was a 15th-century wickerwork fish trap. The trap had stones inside it to weigh it down and wooden pegs to secure it to the bottom of the moat. Previously, it was only suspected that fishing took place in the moat and, finally, here was evidence that it actually took place.

CHAPTER 7

A day in the life

An average day in the life of the Tower has, in many ways, remained the same over hundreds of years – and yet at the same time, each day is unique. The day starts officially when the Tower gates are unlocked at six o-clock in the morning. Yeoman Warders or 'Beefeaters' are required to keep guard inside the Tower. Besides their daytime duties, every Yeoman Warder is obliged to be on duty one night every month.

The Tower hosts many exhibitions about the Tower's role through history. This 1840s advertisement features the Tower of London in the background.

A TOP TOURIST SPOT

For tourists, the Tower does not officially open until 9 am (except for Sundays and Mondays when it opens at 10 am). There are many things at the Tower for visitors to see and participate in. The Yeoman Warders are stationed around the Tower and have been trained to answer questions and act as guides to the many tourists.

LIVING HISTORY

The Tower of London holds many exhibitions that concentrate on a particular aspect of its history. There are also regular 'living history' events which usually take place within the school holidays and at weekends. These involve guides dressing up in historical costumes and using parts of the Tower as a stage to tell their

This painting shows a Yeoman Warder taking a group of Victorian children on a tour of the Tower of London. Tourists have been permitted through the Tower since the 16th century.

Whenever a new Yeoman Warder is appointed to work at the Tower of London he has to be sworn in the presence of the other Yeoman Warders by the Constable of the Tower on Tower Green. All of the Yeoman Warders then go to the Yeoman Warders' Club where the new member is toasted. The toast includes the words 'may you never die a warder'. This goes back to the days when Warders could sell their job when they retired. If they died before selling it, then the Constable found a new Warder instead.

stories. There are also costumed events that recreate significant events that took place at the Tower, such as the siege of the Tower of London in 1471 and sword-fighting demonstrations. Christmas is also an interesting

occasion at the Tower where historical festivities are the theme. There are also interactive events at the Tower where, for example, visitors can also help 'prisoners' escape, or vote on what happened to the vanished Princes. The Tower is a popular destination for visiting classes. About 12,000 children visit the Tower each year.

The installation ceremony that takes place every five years involves the ceremonial handing over of keys to the new Constable at the Tower.

GOING OFF WITH A BANG

Guns are brought in especially to conduct fire salutes on important dates throughout the year. These dates include the anniversary of the monarch's coronation, the monarch's birthday (both the 'official' birthday and the real one – in which 62 rounds of ammunition are fired), the State

Opening of Parliament and to acknowledge visits by foreign heads-of-state. The tradition of gun salutes at the Tower was established in about the 1530s.

A UNIQUE WORKFORCE

The day-to-day running of the Tower is handled by the Resident Governor of the Tower. In the past this job was done by the Constable, the monarch's representative at the Tower. The post of Constable still exists but mostly has a ceremonial role these days. A new Constable is appointed every five years. The installation ceremony takes place on Tower Green. The Lord Chamberlain, who represents the monarch, hands the new Constable the keys to the Tower.

The Constable then hands the keys to the Queen's House to the Resident Governor, giving him permission to live there. There are about 150 people working inside the walls of the Tower. They range from working in souvenir shops and in restaurants, to maintenance and cleaning crews to marketing and public relations. Unusual jobs include the Raven Master (who looks after the Tower's ravens) and the Crown Jeweller (who comes to the Tower every January to clean the Crown Jewels).

AN UNUSUAL HOME

Since the Tower was first built, there have been people living there. Likewise today, many of the people who work in the Tower of London also call it home. About 35 Yeoman Warders live in the Tower with their families. Their

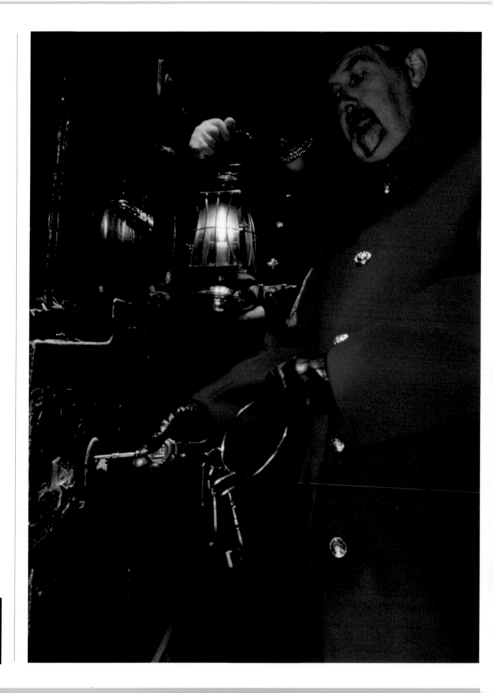

The Tower is locked at the end of each day by the Chief Yeoman Warder (who is accompanied by a military guard). This historic tradition is known as the Ceremony of the Keys.

Tales & customs – IN THE DRINK

On February 18, 1478, the Duke of Clarence was allegedly drowned in a barrel of Malmsey wine at the Tower of London. The obvious reason for this might appear to be that he fell in drunk, but this wasn't the case. Instead, it is likely that he was executed on the orders of his brother, King Edward IV for alleged involvement in several major conspiracies against the King. The Duke's unusual death has been immortalised by Shakespeare in his play, Richard III.

smart-looking townhouses face onto Tower Green. Other officials such as the Governor, Deputy Governor and the Chief Exhibitor of the Crown Jewels also live inside the walls of the Tower.

Most of the residents of the Tower live in the Casemates, which are buildings set into the walls of the Tower. The Resident Governor lives in the Queen's House on Tower Green. The Tower also has a resident

The Captain of the Guards is the most senior of all the Yeoman Warders. He is also known as the Chief Yeoman Warder.

chaplain. The chaplain holds services at St. Peter ad Vincula, the chapel within the Tower. There are regular Sunday services as well as special services. The chaplain also takes part in special occasions such as the Beating of the Bounds. Members of the public are welcome to any of these services.

BEHIND THE SCENES

The Tower of London is usually closed to the public at 5 pm in the winter and at 6 pm during the rest of the year. The Tower is then locked up with the ancient Ceremony of the Keys. Afterwards, the Yeoman Warders can relax in their own private club – the oldest club in London, in fact. The Victorian-style interior of the club is decorated with regimental heraldry on the walls, along with original newspaper and magazine cartoons military themes, especially those that relate to the Tower. Such interesting things as the framed signature of Rudolf

Hess and various plaques presented to the Yeoman Warders by various military and police organisations from all over the world.

One of the main roles of Yeoman Warders today is to act as guides to visiting tour parties.

CHAPTER 8

Preserving the past

T he Tower of London is one of the most important buildings in British history and a very important part of the London tourist industry. Over two million people visit it every year. This means that looking after the buildings and interiors in the Tower of London is incredibly important. This care and maintenance is handled by an organisation called Historic Royal Palaces.

NATURAL THREATS

The Tower faces several threats from the environment. Changes in air temperature can cause damage to the masonry on the outside of buildings. This is known as 'thermal movement'. Water is also a problem. Many of the stones and bricks used in the buildings within the Tower are porous. This means that they allow a little bit of water in. This water can damage both the surface and inside of the stone. Inside the buildings, light can cause damage to walls and furniture. Organic materials like wood, fabric and paint can fade if they are exposed to light. Insects and beetles, such as the Deathwatch beetle, can also cause damage to wood.

The Crown Jeweller cleans the Crown Jewels once a year. In this photo he is cleaning the beautiful Imperial State Crown.

CAR POLLUTION

The Tower is situated next to a busy road in the centre of London. The vibrations from the heavy vehicles that pass by have an effect on the structure of the Tower. Exhaust fumes not only make dust, which coats the Tower (making it harder to clean), but also contribute to making rain slightly acid.

PROTECTING THE PAST

The outside of the Tower sometimes needs to be cleaned to prevent damage to the stone and bricks. Ordinary cleaning systems can destroy the historic fabric of a building, so specialist techniques are used. Structural engineers also monitor the condition of the buildings

Tales & customs – LOST LOVE/LOST LIVES

The interior walls of the Beauchamp Tower are covered in inscriptions left by the prisoners kept there in the years when the Tower was still a prison. On the walls of one of the state prison rooms are the words, JANE, JANE, alleged to have been carved by Lord Guildford Dudley during his imprisonment and separation from his wife (Lady Jane Grey), who was at the same time a prisoner elsewhere in the Tower. Both were eventually executed at the Tower in 1554, (see p. 29).

themselves and must decide whether they need reinforcing. Inside, the conservation team needs to test light levels, temperature, humidity and ventilation, as well as monitoring dust levels. Delicate items such as textiles and paintings need specialist care. Historic Royal Palaces has a laboratory that provides scientific advice on conservation issues – testing the strength of materials, checking light and heat ageing, and dust monitoring. Damage to historic paintings and materials are also monitored and conservation repairs are carried out when necessary.

REPLACING THE PAST

The conservation staff have guidelines that they follow when it comes to repairing or replacing things. If possible, historic

Reconstructions like these that took place at the Royal Chamber of the Wakefield Tower need to be conducted very carefully. All materials must be checked before use to ensure nothing will be damaged in the process.

Replacing stained-glass windows at the Tower can be a painstaking process. Many people are involved to ensure the end result is in keeping with the period of the building.

material should not be removed. All new work should use the right material for the job and all repairs and replacements should be reversible so that the impact on the Tower is minimal.

Glossary

Anglo-Saxons Inhabitants of England (of Germanic descent) from the 5th century AD through to the Norman Conquest in 1066.

Armoury In America an armoury is a place where weapons are made. In the Tower of London it means a place where arms and ammunition are stored.

Barracks A building or set of buildings designed as accommodation for soldiers.

Bastion A projecting part of the wall of a castle. It was meant to defend the wall of the castle on either side.

Beefeater Another term for 'Yeoman Warder' – a security guard at the tower of London.

Campaign Series of military operations with a particular aim or purpose.

Chapel A chapel is slightly different from a church. Chapels tend to small and are can be set aside for either private use or for a small group.

Chartists A group of people in the 19th century who spoke up to parliament with demands for political and social improvements that reflected the needs of the people.

Civil War A war or a conflict fought between two groups within the same country. The war between King Charles II and Parliament under Oliver Cromwell was a civil war.

Concentric Type of medieval castle where the interior is protected by many circles of wall. The Tower of London is an example of a concentric castle.

Constable This is a title normally given to the governor of a royal castle who acts on behalf of the king or queen. It is also the name for any important officer in the royal household. It comes from a French and a Latin word and means 'head of the stable'.

Crusades Series of military campaigns attempted by the British to regain ownership of the Holy Lands from the Muslims.

Defences Way of protecting a town or city against attack, either by constructing physical walls or towers, or in the form of an army of soldiers and weaponry.

Dendrochronology A method of identifying historic dates from the number of rings in tree trunks.

Domesday Book An official record of all the lands and people of England in 1086.

Excavations Finding out more about the history of the site by digging trenches and looking for evidence of past habitation. This digging has to be done carefully to make that all of the evidence is found and recorded.

Execution Killing of a person who has been legally condemned to death.

Exile Person who has been barred from their native country and so lives abroad.

Extortion Obtained by force, threat or unfair means.

Fortress Building or town which has been strengthened against attack.

Fortification Way of strengthening against attack.

Garrison Army of troops stationed in a particular town to defend it from attack.

Illuminations Illustrations that decorate medieval manuscripts.

Incarcerated Imprisoned or confined somewhere.

Keep The Keep is normally the part of the castle that is the strongest and was designed to defend the rest of the castle complex of buildings.

Loops A slit in a wall that is narrow and is cut vertically. It could be used by archers or gunmen inside to defend a building. The inside of the loop was much bigger than the outside so that defenders could fire from different angles.

Londinium Ancient Roman name for the city of London in England.

Menagerie Early versions of modern zoos where wild animals were brought after being captured and were then put on display. It come from the French word 'menage' which means 'household'.

Mint This is a place where coins are made. These are usually official places organised by the State and usually operate under tight security.

Moat Wide ditch filled with water, surrounding and protecting a castle or town.

Monarch Ruler of a country, such as the king or queen.

Mortar Mixture of lime, cement, and and water that is used for holding bricks in place.

Motte and Bailey An early type of castle favoured by the Normans when they first invaded England. The motte was a wooden fortress built on top of an earth mound.

The bailey is a outer wall that surrounds the mound and has other buildings inside it. Most were replaced by stone castles.

Munitions Military weapons and equipment.

Noble Historic term for man or woman who belongs to a high-ranking social class, otherwise known as 'aristocracy'.

Oratory These are usually very small churches or chapels that are used for private worship.

Ordnance A word that describes weapons and ammunition and also the people who are involved in looking after the weapons and ammunition.

Persecution Treated in a cruel or harsh way over a long period of time.

Portcullis This is a strong and heavy gate that can be lowered or raised. It is usually meant to protect the entrance to a fortress.

Ranpart Defensive wall of a castle.

Ransacked Hurried through somewhere, stealing and causing damage in the process.

Rebellion Opposition to authority resulting in an uprising against existing rule. Otherwise known as 'revolt'.

Regiment Permanent army unit.

Salute Showing homage or respect by the firing of guns or cannons.

Scaffold A raised wooden platform on which prisoners were executed. The platform would be built so that the execution could be seen better by those who had come to witness the execution.

Siege This is a military operation in which an army tries to force the surrender of a town or castle. This is usually done either by attacking the town or castle directly or by surrounding it and waiting for the people in the town to run out of supplies.

Traitor A traitor is a person who has acted in a way that hurts or damages to his or her own country or monarch.

Treason The crime of betraying one's country.

Tudor Royal dynasty that held the English throne from Henry VII (1485) until the death of Elizabeth I (1601).

Whitewash A mixture of lime and water used for painting walls white.

Yeoman Warder A security guard at the Tower of London. Also known informally as a 'Beefeater'.

Index

Copyright © ticktock Entertainment Ltd 2005
First published in Great Britain in 2005 by ticktock Media Ltd.,
Unit 2, Orchard Business Centre, North Farm Road, Tunbridge Wells, Kent, TN2 3XF
We would like to thank: Alison Howard, Susan Barraclough, Elizabeth Wiggans and Jenni Rainford for their help with this book.
Printed in Hong Kong. A CIP catalogue record for this book is available from the British Library.

Picture Credits
Alamy: 33; Art Archive: 7R, 10L, 11R, 27L, 27R, 30L, 31R; Bridgeman Art Library: 6L, 16L, 20T, 26, 28L, 29R, 32L, 32R, 40L; Corbis: 18TR, 24BL, 39L, 42, 43B, 44L, 44-5, 45R; Heritage Images: 4BL, 14R; Historic Royal Palace: 9, 20B, 21T, 23B, 24-5, 35, 36, 38L, 39R, 43T; London Aerial Photo Library: 18-19